Francis Amasa Walker

An Oration delivered by Gen'l Francis A. Walker

At the Soldiers' Monument Dedication in North Brookfield, Jan. 19, 1870

Francis Amasa Walker

An Oration delivered by Gen'l Francis A. Walker
At the Soldiers' Monument Dedication in North Brookfield, Jan. 19, 1870

ISBN/EAN: 9783337143435

Printed in Europe, USA, Canada, Australia, Japan

Cover: Foto ©ninafisch / pixelio.de

More available books at **www.hansebooks.com**

ERECTED
BY THE TOWN OF
NORTHBROOKFIELD
IN HONOR OF HER
SOLDIERS WHO LOST
THEIR LIVES IN DEFENCE
OF THEIR COUNTRY
AGAINST THE
REBELLION
1861 – 65

1868.

AN ORATION

DELIVERED BY

GEN'L FRANCIS A. WALKER,

AT THE

Soldiers' Monument Dedication

IN NORTH BROOKFIELD, JAN. 19, 1870.

ALSO THE ADDRESSES OF

His Excellency Wm. Claflin, Gen. Chas. Devens

AND OTHERS, WITH A

BRIEF ACCOUNT OF THE CELEBRATION.

Worcester:
GODDARD & NYE, PRINTERS,
339 Main Street, corner of Front.
1870.

TO THE

WIDOWS, ORPHANS, AND OTHER RELATIVES

OF THE DECEASED,

Whose Patriotism and Sacrifices must ever be the Theme of
Orators and Statesmen,

*This Pamphlet is **Affectionately Inscribed**,*

BY THE COMMITTEE.

CORRESPONDENCE.

WORCESTER, Jan. 22, 1870.

GEN'L FRANCIS A. WALKER:

DEAR SIR:

Pursuant to a vote passed at the Soldiers' Monument Dedication, in North Brookfield, on the 19th instant, the undersigned solicit a copy of the oration delivered by you at that time, for publication, and in this connection please accept our hearty thanks for the great service rendered upon that interesting occasion — service made more than gratuitous by the remembrance of a soldier's widow and children by a noble contribution.

Yours, respectfully,

E. J. RUSSELL,
T. M. DUNCAN,
WM. H. MONTAGUE,
CHARLES ADAMS, JR.
} Committee.

WASHINGTON, D. C., Feb. 1, 1870.

GENTLEMEN:

I am favored with your letter of the 22d ult., requesting a copy of the oration delivered at the Dedication of the Soldiers' Monument at North Brookfield.

I comply with the request in the spirit in which it was made, the same spirit, I am sure, in which the address was prepared and delivered, namely, the earnest desire to do all honor to the patriotic dead of our town.

Very truly yours,

FRANCIS A. WALKER.

CAPT. E. J. RUSSELL,
T. M. DUNCAN, Esq.
W. H. MONTAGUE, Esq.
HON. CHARLES ADAMS, JR.
} Committee.

ORATION.

My Friends:

This is peculiarly the Soldiers' Day. Perhaps we are never less fitted to sympathize with the individual soldier than when indulging the thoughts and feelings proper to the anniversary celebration of some great battle, as when, last summer, thousands were assembled at Gettysburg to commemorate the deeds of that historic field. The dedication of a monument to a distinguished commander, calls up a single majestic figure in which concentres all the glory and renown of a score of battles — from which radiates victory almost as a personal emanation. But an occasion like this which has called us together to-day, brings up the individual soldier in all the variety of his martial experience, march, bivouac, hospital, not less than foughten field, in all the sacredness, and it may be the sorrow, of his domestic relations. This shaft evokes no images of battle as a grand panorama of charging lines and gleaming squadrons, over which presides some heroic spirit, grand and terrible, the genius of desolation, but also of victory. These village commemorations of the fallen brave call up no such pictures of grandeur or terror. They minister nothing to fame, nothing to the love of glory, nothing to the passion of war.

And I cannot but think it fortunate that no name distinguished in arms intrudes upon us here, like a great man at some homely festival, bringing constraint upon the cordial exchanges of neighborly feeling, exacting an unequal share of the attention of the company, and throwing humble merit into the

2

shade. Among the names upon this legend, there are no such differences of rank or reputation as put the least favored at disadvantage. Of all those here commemorated, not one but had served as a private soldier; not one rose to the rank of a commissioned officer. There is something in this which is most congenial to our purpose of paying respect to each and all of the sons of North Brookfield who have fallen in the defense of their country. For one I cannot but be glad that the chance of birth has given to this little town no military officer of distinction to take the lion's share of our remembrance and admiration; no colonel or general to whom belongs pages of eulogy, while the humble soldier who exhibited equal courage, patriotism and self-denial finds only a few lines of praise, perhaps but the simple mention of his name. It is that courage, patriotism and self-denial, in which the general went not a step before the private soldier, which we here commemorate. The accident of military genius, the greater accident of success in war, should be nothing to us on an occasion like this. For our purpose of honoring these men we care not whether they fell in victory or defeat. It makes no difference with their claim on us, or with our affection and gratitude to them. Looking at the sacrifice which each one of them made, from the standpoint of the commander or the historian, and considering merely the importance of his single life to a great army, or the contribution made in his death to the final result of the struggle, it seems small — small indeed as the two mites which make a farthing. Yet looking at the sacrifice from our standpoint to-day, that of patriotic gratitude and neighborly affection, that contribution was as rich and complete as when a Kearney, a Lyon, or a Sedgewick, whose single presence in a fight was worth a thousand men, cast in of his abundance, laying his precious life freely on the altar of his country's liberties.

If there is one thing which we instinctively desire when we have been called to make some great and painful sacrifice, it is to see the fruit of our sacrifice. It makes sorrow and loss twice as hard to bear, to know that they are in vain; to know that what we valued most and loved best have been thrown utterly away. Those dreadful days are still too deeply impressed on your memories that you should need to be reminded how, for two years, every quick succeeding shock of war was rendered more distressing and terrible by the consciousness that so much blood and treasure were being wasted through the systematic misdirection of effort, and by the ignorance and incompetence of our commanders.

So frequent and so distressing became these disasters that the sentiment to which allusion has been made did not merely add to the poignancy of private grief. It became a great element in the problem of the war; it discouraged enlistments; it terribly weakened the forces in the field. Young men declined to enter the army because there was no assurance that they would not be led to slaughter by drunken or worthless officers. It was, perhaps, inevitable; but it was none the less wrong. The duty of a man to serve and save his country does not depend on any such conditions. No citizen has a right to make terms for his own life, when the life of the nation is in peril. If such a plea were to be accepted, it would become the ample excuse for every delinquency, and no man would find the time when he was so fully satisfied of the competency of his country's generals, and the correctness of the military or political principles on which the war was to be waged, quite to see his way clear to enlist. What would have become of us and the great cause of human liberty and republican government had not there been found men who did not count the risk or criticise their orders; but buffeted the dark, cold waves of defeat and disaster without hope for themselves, and sank beneath them without one complaining cry?

Disasters will occur in war. "The general that has never made a mistake has fought few battles," said Washington. But without any mistakes made, defeat may come to the best appointed and best commanded army, by the mysterious

chances of battle, or through the operation of general but
remote and inappreciable causes. Those who will fight only on
the winning side and under the victorious commander, must
enlist after the war and not at its beginning. Nay, it often
becomes a necessity of national existence that a people shall
enter upon a protracted contest without veteran troops and
accomplished leaders; to trust to bloody and costly experi-
ments, a long succession, it may be, of defeats and disasters,
to train the troops and the commanders who shall achieve
the final victory. It is very hard, of course, but the only
alternative is national dishonor or dissolution, and between
the two no true man will hesitate; and no one is excused on
account of his very natural and proper dislike to become one
of the victims of such an experiment. It is pleasanter, vastly,
to march to victory under a skilled and resolute general, with
high hopes and the courage that is inspired of confidence in a
commander. But it is even more a duty, sometimes, to go without shrinking into what you know to be not a battle but a
butchery. The responsibility of the event rests with others.
Your way is plain. To refuse to discharge your duty because
of the certain destruction which attends it, would be to sacrifice
interests far more precious than life; and probably in the end
to sacrifice ten lives for one that might be saved by such an
abandonment of obligation and honor.

In our case, this hardship was aggravated and prolonged
almost beyond endurance by having to submit to these harrow-
ing experiences, not for the instruction of commanders well
selected and giving a reasonable promise of profiting by their
rebuffs and defeats; but for the sake of exhibiting successively
the hopeless incompetence of a half-score of military pretenders,
whom, if instinct were as strong in men as it is in horses and
dogs, we should have known at sight to be imposters.

What sad, wretched days those were! What a trial of our
faith and constancy! What a burden of fear and sorrow!
Painful enough for the soldier in the field; more painful still

9

for fathers and mothers and wives at home. But, I say again, this made no difference with the question of duty. The more unfortunate the country in its commanders, the more need to have brave and devoted soldiers. Do you plead that this is a hard saying — who shall bear it? I answer, your soldiers bore it, the much-enduring men who, through years weary marching and bloody fighting, hardly ever saw one day of triumph; who, beaten again and again, without any fault of theirs, insulted and betrayed on the right hand and on the left, still stood by their colors; following them, victorious or beaten, yes, followed them to such an end as these comrades and friends of ours whom we bury anew to-day.

But I will not add to the distress of mourning friends by dwelling upon so painful a theme. Strangely enough, and fortunately, in that most inexcusable of all the massacres into which the Union troops were led by incompetent and bewildered generals — the melancholy and mysterious affair at Ball's Bluff — not one soldier from North Brookfield lost his life. In that terrible initiation, the regiment with which at the time all our hopes and interests were connected, lost blood almost to fainting; its bravest officers, its best men, fell in that dark and bloody strife; and the 15th regiment and our company F returned to their camp at Poolesville, only the shadow of what they were when they marched out from among us, accompanied by our acclamations and our prayers; yet not one of our own boys was found among the victims. It cannot help seeming strange to look upon that tablet, and reflect that in all the long list of the fallen there should not be a single representative of the battle which, at the time, so powerfully moved us; which formed the theme of so much comment, and cast such a gloom over this community during the whole of that long and wearisome winter. How little we then appreciated the real proportions of the struggle on which we had entered! Would our courage and patriotism have held good, had it then been told us that battle after battle should follow in fierce succession, and that the tidings of sons fallen in fight should on ten different occasions thereafter be borne to the homes of North Brookfield?

Generally speaking, however, it may be said that our soldiers were fortunate, since they must die, in the time and manner of their death. More than our fair share, when we consider how many were the misconceptions and miscarriages of the war, fell under circumstances that caused us to feel that their death was not in vain — fell on days when the forces of treason and slavery were broken and driven by the patriotic valor of a loyal and liberty-loving army.

It is a surprising fact that among the thirty-one soldiers from this town, who fell the victims of battle and disease, are found the representatives of nineteen different regiments, belonging to as many as seven States. How strangely this indifference, manifested in the later years of the war, as to the circumstances of service, contrasts with the sentiment which animated the North Brookfield soldiers of 1861, when we united with two neighboring towns to form Company F of the 15th regiment! Why, in those days, hardly one of our number would have thought that he could bring his mind to enlist in a strange regiment, or even in another company from that to which his schoolmates and his townsmen belonged. But we well know, how soon the feeling wore off under the teaching of actual service; and that soldiers became almost strangely indifferent to the accidents of circumstance and surroundings, having learned that war is war anywhere and anyhow; that in its tremendous experience the petty fact of previous acquaintance goes for very little; that in the hardships and dangers of campaign, men lay the foundations of far deeper and more intimate friendships than are possible in this peaceful and self-indulgent life of ours.

But the number which has been mentioned as the number to which our dead soldiers belonged, does not express the full measure of that scattering which sent our sons and brothers to fight on almost every field where liberty and union were battled for. In addition to these, I find that this town was represented in

eighteen other regiments and batteries of the loyal army, making
a total of thirty-seven organizations borne upon the military roll
of North Brookfield. Separated thus widely, it is not strange
that of the comparatively small number of fourteen who died of
wounds received at the hands of the enemy, not less than nine
important battles of the war are given as the place of death,
while still another perished in the advance guard of Sherman's
army in his famous march to the sea. In only two actions did
North Brookfield have to mourn more than a single loss. At
Cold Harbor fell Nathan S. Dickinson; at Piedmont, George
S. Prouty; at Petersburg, on the 30th of September, Lyman H.
Gilbert; at the first Fredericksburg, David S. Moulton; at
Cedar Creek, John Henry Jenks; at Winchester, James P.
Coolidge; and at Poole's Station, by treacherous and cowardly
assassination, William Clark. But at Spottsylvania we lost both
George L. Sherman and Lyman D. Winslow; while in the
dark woods that fringe the banks of Antietam Creek, fell in one
bloody and terrible half-hour, Henry R. Bliss, Joseph C. Fretts
and Charles Perry.

Our experience as a town fully bears out the observation that,
despite all the pictured horrors of battle, more perish in war by
the stroke of disease than by sword or bullet. Sixteen of these
men died, not in the flush of health and courage, not in the
tumult of the onset, amid the cheers of charging lines, but by
painful and lingering disease, in distant hospitals; some, alas!
in the hands of cruel and vindictive enemies. Quite otherwise
than as we might have supposed, these soldiers made their beds
of death closer together than the fourteen who fell in battle.
Peter Devlin, indeed, died at Nashville, John A. Huges at
Philadelphia, Lyman Tucker at Alexandria, Alonzo E. Pellet at
Vicksburg, Thomas Griffin in the confederate prison at Salis-
bury, and Charles Ashby returned to die among his friends in
his own home. But of the remainder, four died at Newbern,
that charnel house of brave men; two more on the same ship in
the same brief voyage; while not less than four from the town

perished, the victims of rebel brutality, in the prison pens of
Andersonville.

Perhaps no part of our loss is harder to get over than this
last. If anything could justify sentiments of undying hatred
toward all who participated in the slaveholders' rebellion, it was
the treatment of our defenceless prisoners. Our faltering human
thought can conceive but one reason why a God of mercy
should have permitted such hellish cruelties ; that slavery, about
to perish from the earth, condemned by the conscience of the
race, driven by the steady advance of human enlightenment to
a last desperate contest for existence, and already even in its
death-struggle, should raise its own hideous monument of terror
and shame, and carve thereon its own epitaph of everlasting
infamy. Andersonville, with its 14,000 graves of martyred men,
dying by a death whose tortures tongue cannot utter nor
thought conceive, deliberately and malignantly exposed and
starved until reason or life gave way ; Andersonville, where, as
a confederate commission officially reported, out of 30,000
prisoners, 8,008 died in the two months of July and August,
1864 ; Andersonville, where only death was merciful, and an
unnamed and unmarked grave was the best hope of the suffering
patriot ; Andersonville will ever remain, while history utters its
solemn voice, or the dim, receding echoes of tradition are heard
along the ages, the true and just and perfect portraiture of
human slavery. It was slavery that crowded our brothers and
our sons into those foul prison pens ; it was slavery that denied
them every comfort and decency of life ; it was slavery that
drew that devilish dead line around that camp of horrors ; it was
slavery that dealt out the vile and scant provision which could
not sustain life, but only prolong agony ; slavery built and
filled and guarded those dreadful stockades ; slavery, in its last
desperate struggle, abandoning all concessions to public opinion,
throwing off all disguises, fighting in its own peculiar spirit, and
doing its own proper work upon the dear bodies of our brothers
and our sons. The slavery that did these deeds of hell, was the

same slavery, nothing else and nothing worse, with which we compromised, and for which we found excuses; of which we took southside views, and at whose dictation we surrendered, one by one, the chartered privileges of our freedom! Cursed, forever accursed, be the thought and name of human slavery! Shame, eternal shame, to every one who defends the monstrous wrong to man and insult to God!

Such and so many were the losses to North Brookfield in the war of the rebellion. The contribution which we were called on to make was no greater than that of many of our neighboring towns, of thousands of villages all over the face of this stricken land. Nor do we wish to claim any superior merit of courage or devotion for these our friends and brothers over the fallen brave of any other town or section. We are satisfied to praise our own, recognizing gladly and gratefully the worth and deserving of all who fought beneath the same flag with them or fell on the same fields of battle. We have the right to speak well of our own. These men we believe to have been good soldiers and true men, all of them. With a single exception hereafter to be mentioned, I do not know that any discredit rests upon the military record or personal character, in the field, of a single one of them. Speaking broadly but conscientiously, the men we commemorate, to-day, were brave, capable and devoted soldiers, well worthy of their place in the noblest army the world ever saw, and well worthy of lasting remembrance and honor among us. And it must not be forgotten that simply to be a good soldier, to maintain an unblemished record and to keep the respect and confidence of comrades and commanders, in all the trying scenes and circumstances of war, is to prove one's self possessed of a very high order of manhood. It is not like simply avoiding social censure at home, which a man may do who has nothing positive and strong about him — perhaps is the more likely to do because he has nothing strong or positive about him. But merely to do one's duty with an army in the field requires the constant display of qualities, which, whenever

3

shown in peaceful life, attract universal attention and excite the highest admiration. How many a man has by a single act of courage and devotion redeemed an otherwise questionable character and wasted life.

But in war, especially such a war as ours, acts of heroism made up the almost daily life of the soldier. Probably not one of the audience not himself a soldier, ever suffered, on any occasion of his life, as our brave boys, day and night, from month to month, in the terrible winter campaigns into which they were driven, in defiance of reason and nature, by the impatience of the country and the miserable interference of the politicians at Washington. Probably not one of you ever once knew what it was to be as hungry as — I will not say those who pined and starved in southern prisons — but as the majority of our soldiers frequently were on the march when supplies were short. You have felt the heat almost unendurable at times, but what do you think of marching in file for twenty-five miles on such a day as the 14th of August, 1864, the sun never going in for a moment, the dust standing twenty feet high in a dense column that could be seen for miles, and men lying dead from exhaustion on both sides of the road? As for giving any one who has not experienced it an idea of the physical agony of going for days together without sleep, save as it could be found lying in a dusty or a frozen road, while the broken down artillery horses stopped for a moment's rest, or snatched in the intervals of skirmish and battle, with shells plunging to right or left unheard or unheeded — I despair of it.

Thus, putting aside the necessity of occasionally encountering the most appaling dangers, such and other frequent and almost unceasing discomforts are the lot of the soldier in the discharge of his duty. Nor must it be thought that these hardships are necessary to every soldier, whether he would escape them or not, and that therefore they are borne as things inevitable are borne. It is always entirely possible for a soldier to shirk if he has the mind to do it. It is not necessary to recount the hundred artifices and pretences by which men contrive to get out of fight, off from picket, or into hospital, in order to show that the soldier who does good duty, does it because he would rather encounter danger, fatigue and pain than be known to his comrades and his officers as a shirk. And because the hardships and trials of army service are such as they are, and are at the same time in a certain and in a high sense voluntary, it is true that for one simply to have the record of a good soldier, simply to discharge the regular duties of camp and outpost, of march and battle, is to deserve high praise. The more showy qualities of soldiership, the chance of performing some brilliant exploit, or the accident of an especial military gift, added little, if anything, to the real claim of the citizen-soldier upon the remembrance and gratitude of his neighbors and friends. It is this ordinary and average performance of duty, involving, as it did, for each and every good soldier, just as much courage, fidelity and devotion as were displayed by the most brilliant and gifted corps commander, which we wish especially to recognize and commemorate here.

It is for this reason, I said at the beginning, that it was a matter almost of congratulation that these men were so nearly equal and uniform in their rank and fortunes. And for the same reason it is, perhaps, better not to dwell at length here upon the individual merit of particular soldiers, although among these dead are some who were conspicuous, even among the faithful, for their resolution and cheerfulness. It is better that they should remain equal in the grave, for the sacrifice of home and hopes and life was the same to each ; and after all, it might be that, when the praise had been distributed with an impartial hand according to desert, as man judgeth, there might be some, least praised and most scantily remembered, who, as God seeth, were most deserving of all, and contributed more, out of their poverty, toward the establishment of Union and freedom than many a belaced and bestarred brigadier.

But while refraining thus from any attempt to characterize the individual services of our North Brookfield soldiers, it would be doing injustice to my own feelings, and I believe, to yours, to withhold a single word in especial recognition of the inexhaustible cheerfulness and the undaunted courage of Charles Perry, the very ideal of a soldier of the Young Guard; the profound and thoughtful patriotism of Holman, who died a veteran soldier at the age of eighteen; the neat and graceful soldiership of Charles Ashby; the marked conscientiousness of Gilbert; the many high qualities of James Knight and John Henry Jenks, good citizens as well as good soldiers; the long and faithful services of Nathan S. Dickinson; the frank and impetuous character of McCarty, fair representative as he was of the Irish-American soldier; the manly bearing of Sergeant Potter, in his single, brief campaign; and the courage, proved on more than one bloody field, of Fretts and Coolidge, Clark and Sherman. Nor can the most rapid enumeration omit to acknowledge the costly contribution of that father among us who gave two brave boys to die for their country, one on that field of high renown, the first Fredericksburg — the other in the prison-pens of Andersonville. What one of the propertied men of North Brookfield has paid a war tax like this? May the sympathy of his fellow-citizens be to the father in place of his sons; and may a just pride in their courage and devotion assuage the regrets and comfort the loneliness of age.

I have spoken of fourteen of our North Brookfield soldiers who fell honorably in battle and died of lingering wounds; and again of sixteen who, with not less patriotism and devotion, nor deserving your honor and gratitude less, gave up their lives in hospital, burning with fever contracted in the pestilential marshes of the South, or wasting away in a long and painful decline, induced by the almost unprecedented hardships and exposures of the war. But this does not make the tale of our losses complete. Another there was who went out from us and came not back to us. The record against his name was not an honorable one. The cause and manner of his death were painful and shameful as any known to the criminal law of war.

Yet the surviving soldiers of North Brookfield have voted unanimously to have his name placed upon this monument, and I can honestly and freely say that my own judgment approves this decision. William F. Hill, of the 20th Massachusetts regiment, suffered as a deserter at Brandy Station, Va., on the 28th of August, 1863. In recording his name with those of brave and loyal men who fell nobly fighting in the front of battle, we mean no disrespect to their memory. We intend no apology for the grievous crime of desertion, which richly merits its penalty of death. This action — questionable enough on a mere statement of it, and demanding an ample explanation, or else this monumental stone were better not raised at all — has been taken in the full conviction of all his comrades in the field and his neighbors at home, that William F. Hill, in that for which he suffered, was not properly and fully an accountable person.

Had there been a just representation of the case, and a calm investigation been made into the competency of the convicted man, he would probably have been discharged from the guard house and the service. But the time was not favorable to nice discriminations. For two years we had carried on a war without adequate discipline. The mistaken lenity — one is tempted to call it the maudlin philanthropy — of the authorities at Washington, rendered it perfectly hopeless to inflict the death penalty for the worst crimes of which a soldier can be guilty — desertion in the face of the enemy, cowardice in action, sleeping upon post. No matter how clear the case or imperative the necessity of punishment, pardon was just as sure to follow conviction as day to follow night. So monstrous had this wrong become, so plain and incontestible the injury resulting from it, that, after the battle of Gettysburg, the new commander of the Potomac army, strong in the reputation acquired on that glorious field, and supported by the military as well as the civil opinion of the country, was enabled to enforce the penalty of death for desertion. Now, when the principle of lenity has been long and grossly abused, the first exercises of severity will generally be excessive. It is almost inevitably so; and the fault belongs, on any just survey of the facts, not to those who have undertaken to restore the law and reform abuses, but to those who, by their ill-considered clemency, have made this a work of great difficulty.

At the time to which I refer, the edict having gone forth that desertion was to be treated as a crime and deserters to be punished, the few weeks during which the Potomac army rested on the Rappahannock in the summer of 1863 witnessed arrests, trials and executions altogether unknown before or since. In their zeal to obey orders, and perhaps, also to secure rewards, provost marshals arrested, among others, some whom it would have been wisdom and humanity to overlook; in their sense of the monstrous wrong which the army had suffered from indiscriminate lenity toward offenders, court martials convicted in some cases where otherwise they might have seen occasion to doubt; and in a sort of self-distrust, a feeling that if they gave way at all to the rage for pardoning, it would become impossible to carry out the stern determination at which they had arrived, the authorities charged with reviewing the proceedings and confirming the sentences of the courts, failed in some instances to exercise that discrimination which, under circumstances which brought less strain upon their firmness, they would have exercised. I was personally cognizant of more than one case of hardship, where, although the accused was technically guilty, the degree of crime was so small, and the mitigating circumstances so numerous and powerful, that the execution of the sentence was an act of mistaken policy, if not of actual injustice. I think the bravest man I ever saw die was shot for desertion, a hundred yards in front of my tent, during this bloody season.

The case of William F. Hill is believed to be of this description. My recollection is that I drew and signed the order which assembled the court martial for his trial. The proceedings of

the court passed through my hands going up for review, and
the sentence of death was made official to the general of division
by my signature. Yet in neither of these instances did it occur
to me that it was a fellow-townsman who was being sentenced to
an ignominious death. Had Hill belonged to the 15th regiment
— certainly if to Company F — the name must have struck me
familiarly and awakened inquiry. Had I known who it was
upon whom the sentence was passed, I believe I do not overrate
my credit with the general commanding the army, in saying that
I could have prevented the execution, by representing at headquarters the character and circumstances of the prisoner. As
it was, the name merely attracted no attention; and it was not
until long after the volley of the provost guard had returned
dust to dust, that I learned the fate of William F. Hill.

It is in the conviction that this one of our North Brookfield
soldiers was only technically guilty of the crime of desertion,
which tens of thousands committed wilfully and wickedly,
flagrantly and frequently, yet wholly escaped punishment; and
that the character of his mind and the circumstances of his life
were such as to reduce his responsibility for such an act to very
narrow limits; it is in this conviction, with the earnest desire to
do what may yet remain to undo the wrong which was unin-
tentionally committed, that we place his name upon this
monument, among the names of men who fell gallantly in
the front of battle, or died of disease incurred in the high and
honorable discharge of duty. And we believe that the hearts
and consciences of all present here, to-day, will approve and
confirm this decision.

What, my friends, are the lessons of this hour? Why have
we reared this shaft upon our village green? What have we
set it to show and teach? This stone certainly will not teach
the love of war and of glory. Standing before a monument to
some illustrious commander, whose name sounds still like a
trumpet blast on the ears of a nation, there are few men of bold
and generous spirit who can remain unmoved by the recollection

of his exploits and the contemplation of his fame. It is no credit
to a man to be opposed to war because he has not nerve and
pluck enough for its fierce contests; nor is he a noble lover of
peace who has no apprehension of what is splendid and brilliant
in battle. Who could stand before the monument of Nelson
without being filled and thrilled and overpowered with the
greatness and the glory of a life and a death so superb, so
magnificent? In such a presence we forget how much war
costs; the terrible tax of sorrow it lays upon unoffending and
uninterested millions; the awful waste of human life and social
power which it involves; the debt and beggary it entails upon
unborn generations. No wonder such a man as Southey — mild,
peaceful and benign, but a thoroughly manly man — was carried
away by his theme when he wrote the life of Nelson. Who,
indeed, can contemplate that life of glory, growing ever brighter
and brighter, to its close, and expiring at last in such a radiance
of splendor — death itself crowning life with the perfect fullness
of honor and fame — and not feel that such a life were worth a
thousand deaths, and such a death worth a thousand ordinary
lives?

But when we stand before such a memorial stone as this we
dedicate to-day, we realize what war means; we see here what
glory costs. There were thirty young men in this remote and
peaceful village who must die for nothing else than that there
was war — husbands, sons and brothers; what a war tax North
Brookfield had to pay! And yet hardly a village within our
land but made an equal contribution of its youthful blood and
strength. Had the struggle been for territory, or commercial
supremacy, or for glory, or for "satisfaction" for any real or
imagined wrong, what an awful price this would have been to
pay! How unworthy every object in comparison but human
liberty and national unity!

Yet this is war. And it is right and wholesome that this
stone should rise in perpetual testimony, a witness sparing or
ceasing not to the desolations and the misery of war. So may

it be with us; and while we grudge not that which we did and suffered for union and liberty, may we fully resolve that nothing but an equal necessity shall ever again call for such contributions and sacrifices. Let this monument to our deceased brothers keep always before our minds this lesson of the horror and mischief of war. Let it remain a perpetual motive for peace and international good-will. Let it instruct our youth who themselves shall have known nothing of those distressful days of anguished partings and heart-breaking news of battle, or having known do but dimly remember — let it instruct them in a wholesome dread of war, not from any personal fear of what might come to themselves out of it, but from simple, human, Christian compassion for the sorrow and bereavement which war always brings in its train. And, as our minds are imbued with a literature all aglow with the romance of campaign and battle; as we catch the thrilling strains of martial enthusiasm from the poet, the orator, and (O hideous incongruity !) the preacher of Christ's gospel of peace, let this monumental stone teach us what war truly is.

God grant that the mournful eloquence of these soldiers' monuments, rising as they do in every village and hamlet of this broad land, may so impress their lesson on the minds and hearts of our people that the craft of statesmen and the selfish zeal of demagogues shall evermore be powerless to draw the nation from the paths of peace. Rarely gifted in our seclusion from the irritating controversies of European diplomacy; with no fatal heritage of dissention and hate; with no nation in the same hemisphere which does not exist by our sufferance, and with none in the old world that can hope to get gain or glory out of us; with no complaint against any that would justify a single day of war, and with the cordial sympathy of two of the most powerful nations of the future; with greatness and wealth unparalleled and unbounded, secured to us by our geographical position and endowments; and with our own unity firmly established by the pathetic sacrifice which we here commemorate,

4

why should we ever again draw the sword? What cause of complaint can ever exist which it will not be possible, with a spirit of conciliation and forbearance, to adjust without loss of power, reputation or self-respect? Is it conceivable that folly and madness shall ever prevail so far as to render it necessary for us again to send out our sons and brothers to die by hundreds and thousands on distant fields? Is it possible that a future generation shall be called to found another such monument as this, to commemorate another company of gallant men, sent from this bright world in the pride of strength and youth?

And if the war of the rebellion was indeed to be our *last* war as a nation, if this pathetic sacrifice is never again to be repeated, how appropriate and just that such a monument as this should signalize and commemorate deeds destined to be so grandly historical; virtue and patriotism so well worthy to be held up to the admiration and imitation of succeeding generations more fortunate than ourselves.

And, firstly, this monument represents the idea of supreme duty to country. Let this be the lesson it shall teach to us and to the generations that follow us. It has frequently been said that prior to the outbreak of the rebellion, Americans hardly realized that they had a country, or, at least, that they were citizens of a nation. The miserable chicane of national politics had indeed not seldom aroused the passions and enlisted the sympathies of the whole people; but politics have little enough to do with patriotism; many of the patriotic people in the world have had no politics; and it was literally true that only by the quadrennial wrangle for power and place did we know ourselves as citizens of a great nation. We were not even proud of our country. Conceit and vanity, indeed, we had, and quite enough of them. A boastfulness that was offensive, and a jealous and angry sensitiveness that betrayed the want of self-respect, were among the characteristics which justly excited the ridicule of foreigners. But we do not live and move and have our being in the honor and power of our country, as Englishmen or

Frenchmen have. The several States had charge of all the concerns which belong to social and domestic life. The national government was to the daily thoughts of our citizens hardly less a myth, than the wretched doctrine of secession and state rights sought to make it out to be in law.

Fortunately, when the great trial came, it was found that other causes had preserved the vital instinct of patriotism. The heroic impulses and forces of the revolutionary time were still strong enough to save the nation. The traditions of faith and courage and devotion availed, even in the absence of a present culture, to command the energies of the people in the hour of its great agony. Never did "blood tell" more distinctly and emphatically. No sooner was the first gun fired, than the whole nation returned to the feelings and sentiments of its early life. The names of the past were found to be more potent than the forces of the present.

It is to maintain and cherish this sentiment of supreme obligation which was happily found to exist, though latent, in the hearts of our countrymen, in the hour of our peril, but which we had hardly a right to expect to find — it is to make this sentiment a part of the future education of our people, so that the duty shall be alike proclaimed by all and accepted by all, that such monuments as these should be founded all over the land. Nor do we wish simply to insure that another trial, when it comes to the nation, shall find the traditions of loyalty and patriotism as lively and strong as they were at the outbreak of the rebellion. We would deepen and intensify these feelings, and impress this great lesson by all possible urgency and frequency of precept and illustration. so that, should we ever again be called to enter on such a desperate struggle for national existence, it shall not be said to our shame that the stream of volunteering ran dry in two years of war; that, instead of bidding for places, we came to bid for men ; that we exchanged the eager emulation of 1861-2 for the tardiness and reluctance of 1863-4.

I speak plainly. No reflection is intended on those who accepted the bounty of the federal government, or of their state or town, on entering the service. When such premiums are offered, he would be over-scrupulous who should refuse them. It was hard enough to support a family on the scanty wages of a soldier, paid in dishonored and depreciated paper, with all the help which the soldier was likely to obtain from any quarter. The shame was that it became first difficult, and then impossible to obtain good men, or finally any kind of men, on the most liberal terms which patriotism or the fear of the draft could offer. "Seven hundred dollars and a cow" is rather a high price for a raw recruit; and this monument and such monuments as these will be cheap in a money point of view — to urge no other or nobler consideration — if they shall so instruct the rising generation in the sentiments of devotion to country, and of manly self-respect, that it will never be necessary again to eke the quotas of our New England towns by coaxing young boys to enlist, or enticing feeble-minded youth from the safe retreats which the charity of the State has provided.

These are the sentiments of one soldier, and he believes he may add in behalf of the soldiers of North Brookfield, "So say we all of us." May this monumental stone so teach and so preach, that whenever again the life of the nation is at stake, there shall be, from first to last, an eager emulation among the young men of the country for the posts of honor and danger, and such a social sentiment among all classes and sexes that no one can forbear to answer the call for men, unless his engagements of family or business are such as — not in his own opinion, but in that of the community — to debar him, positively, from the privilege.

Secondly, this monument stands as a token of personal remembrance, personal affection and personal gratitude, on the part of the citizens of this town, toward each and all of the deceased, fallen as they have in our behalf and in our stead. By this sculptured stone we acknowledge our obligation to

remember and honor these men individually and personally.
Nor let us think that this is a matter of course. The claim they
have on us is not to be satisfied by vague declarations about
liberty and union, by panegyrics on the proclamation of emancipation and the fifteenth amendment of the constitution, by
general tributes to the long-suffering courage and devotion of
our troops, nor even by hearty admiration for the average or the
ideal soldier of the republic. It was not "the cause" that bled
from wounds or burned with fever. It was not the cause which
made long and wearisome marches, which stood on picket dark
and stormy nights, which went hungry many a day, and slaked
its thirst at slimy pools from which dumb creatures turned
in disgust. It was not the cause that suffered exile for years
from all that makes life pleasant, and finally lay down to die
upon the trampled sod of the battlefield, or amid the rude
discomforts of a crowded hospital. Neither was it the ideal
American soldier who did these things. Mighty little, indeed,
did the ideal soldier do, anyway. He made his appearance
principally in the pages of *Harper's Weekly*, and performed his
feats of daring almost exclusively in the diaries of army
chaplains. It was not even the average soldier, rough, brave
and capable, who won our liberties. It was done by actual
soldiers, veritable men of flesh and blood, from real northern
and western homes; some of them, no doubt, not a bit better
than they ought to be. But still they did it. Many of them
had faults enough, but they died in our place; weaknesses
enough, but they upheld and saved the state.

It is very cheap and easy to go into raptures over a cause,
forgetting individual men, their merits and their claims. It is
very pleasant and natural to acknowledge obligations to our
patriotic defenders in the abstract, while cherishing a sort of
contemptuous pity for some of them whom we fancy not to have
been quite as wise, or correct, or successful in worldly matters
as ourselves. By no such vague and impersonal acknowledg-
ments shall we discharge our duty to these dead. We owe

them, singly and individually, our friendly remembrance, our charitable construction of every fault or failing; our heartfelt gratitude, personally and by name, for all they did and all they endured; our sympathy, our society and our aid, in all readiness and cheerfulness, for every unhappy dependant left to mourn this loss.

I have not had the spirit to talk to you to-day of the fifteenth amendment, of emancipation and reconstruction, of the lessons and the results of the war, or of any of the themes which are popular upon occasions like this. My heart has been too full of the thoughts of these men, my playmates and comrades. Let the politicians settle it among themselves, how to secure the fruits of all this sacrifice and all this effort. Nay, at another time and elsewhere it will be our duty and privilege as citizens and patriots, to provide that not one drop of this precious blood shall be lost, but that, by the gracious blessing of our fathers' God, this mournful sacrifice of manly courage, of tender affections and youthful hope, shall minister to the dignity, purity and freedom of the state which they loved and for which they died. But, to-day, let proclamations and constitutional amendments, reconstruction and suffrage pass, and let us meet around this monumental stone, neighbors and friends, it may be also fathers, brothers and sons, mourning the patriotic death of these good men and true; lifting up our voices together in testimony to their courage, their generosity and their faithfulness; and promising ourselves and each other that so long as we live and this sculptured granite shall rise among us, we will reverently think upon them, tenderly speak of them, and hold them up to the honor and imitation of our sons.

And now I come to a portion of my remarks which, if the object were merely to deliver a smooth and graceful address, and produce a favorable impression, ignoring carefully all that might exact unpleasant reflections or provoke unpleasant recollections, glozing over the surface with fair and fine words, and bringing into light only those aspects of the occasion which are harmonious and agreeable, I should certainly avoid, as I might easily do. But I owe a duty to truth, a duty to these dead, which will not allow me to pass this theme in silence.

There are some men and boys in every village whom our New England civilization does not know what to do with. They do not take kindly to schooling, to meeting-going, or to work. They do not earn, or else they do not save. They offend against propriety in a thousand ways, great and small; and it is well if a sense of strangeness and unsatisfaction does not drive them into offenses against morality or law. They are often in mischief, and always in disgrace with Mrs. Grundy. Men and boys of this stamp our New England civilization does not know how to treat. No form of human civilization ever made so much out of material fitted to its purposes; none ever had so little power to put to use material not according to its patterns. No human society has ever achieved a greater success where ours succeeds; none ever confessed such lamentable failures where ours fails. The degree of that success is the measure of that failure. There is no place for the "ne'er do weel" in New England. If a young man will not be decorous and industrious; if he does not take kindly to the stated means of ordinary and religious education, and especially if he loves not the tea-party and the church fair, society can only shake its head and confess its inability to do anything with him or for him.

Is not this so? Let us put it to our memories and our consciences what single thing we do for a young man who is a little wild, after, it may be, he has rejected one or two well-intentioned offers of tracts, supposed to be particularly suited to his case? In what way do we try to win him on to good, and keep him from going to the bad? How far do we relax the grim severity and prim propriety which we affect, to conciliate his different, and, let us say, much less commendable tastes and fancies? No, we can do nothing for the ne'er-do-weel in New England.

I do not mean to revile our Puritan civilization. It has

accomplished wonderful results. It has achieved magnificent successes. It has created a society not equaled upon earth, or in history. Intelligence, morality, quiet and wealth, beyond the enjoyment of any other people, have been the results of the New England standard of life, and for such success we may well accept all the failure that may be actually necessary in reaching it. But at least we may have a word of charity for those who cannot quite find a place in this order of ours, and so feel themselves of no use in the world, and, perhaps, failing of sympathy, or irritated by too severe reprehension of the venial errors or follies of youth, break away from restraint, and are regarded and treated as the black sheep of our society. Nay, may we not even enquire whether we might not do something for them, and without derogating aught from the noble results of the past, contrive some gracious means to save a part of this wealth of energy, aspiration and passion, which every year goes to waste among us?

The reason for this partial, yet, if partial, most melancholy, failure of our civilization in dealing with the youth of New England, is that the tests which society adopts, though admirably suited for purposes of discipline, and to secure the highest efficiency of the public body as a whole, are intrinsically unjust and often very cruel. All the virtues which public opinion recognizes (and public opinion is, in the fullest and most despotic sense, law in New England), are negative. A man must not, with us, do certain things. If he satisfies society in this, there is no exaggeration in saying that no higher test is applied to his deserving. Now, I admit that it would be well, and a most happy state of things, if every young man with hot blood, high temper and sanguine hopes, were as wise as his father at the age of forty or sixty has become, and if he fully appreciated all the sage and prudential reasons which direct the female public mind of these north-eastern States. But since, by something very like God's appointment, this is not so, it is surely

a great pity that so much spirit, courage and energy is allowed
to run to waste, or to worse.

It is bad enough when society has to reject any portion of its
membership as no longer of any use or worth to itself; but
unfortunately, in our modern civilization, what is thrown aside
as refuse is often the noblest material of society. For I dare
to say in the face of New England propriety, looking into those
cold, gray eyes, and encountering the full effect of that stony
stare, I dare to say that courage and generosity are virtues in
the human character, and not the least among virtues. Society,
to be sure, has little use for them, and so makes but little
account of them. It has arranged all its parts and offices on
the principle that a rational selfishness is the best preservative
of peace, and the most active and efficient agent of progress;
and more romantic notions or less constant forces only disturb
its calculations, and interrupt its regular working. The virtues
it most values are those which best qualify a man to seek and
secure his own interest.

This is not to say that our social conditions make us all
cowardly or selfish, but I do venture to assert, and I appeal to
the consciences of all who hear me, in confirmation, that the
present organization of society utterly ignores those two highest
qualities of the manly character, generosity and courage. No
man needs them to rise in society or hold his place there. All
the influences which surround us tend to disparage these traits
and to develop a spirit of self-carefulness, a disposition to evade
every unpleasant experience or rough encounter, and a high
intentness to coddle and pamper self. Selfishness, by which is
not, of course, meant a miserly penuriousness or a ravening
greed, but an elegant, deferential, smooth-faced and well-spoken
delicacy to self and indifference to others, is eating the heart out
of our modern society. We remain on terms of personal
intimacy for years with men, without a single opportunity to
learn their real disposition; without one occasion offering when

5

society recognizes in us the right to ask, or in them the duty to grant, a single thing which involves hardship or sacrifice.

All this is not aside from my purpose, nor, I think, unworthy of your serious consideration. Men went from among us to the war, of whom we had not been accustomed, measuring ourselves by ourselves and comparing ourselves among ourselves — to think very highly; men who did not take kindly to the artificial manners and the arbitrary morality of "the neighborhood;" wanting somewhat in that sublime quality of looking out for one's self, which is the visible fulfillment of the law; men, some of whom we characterized as their own worst enemies, who had not found a place in this modern order, and for whom society had not yet found much to do; men of whom (I hope it is not an offence against charity to intimate it) it was thought and said, that while wishing them well and with the kindest feelings toward them, society could *afford to spare* much better than others.

We ask not and like not the sympathy, on this occasion, of any man who feels in this way. Speaking for my fellow-soldiers, for the living and for the dead, and for the friends of the men we commemorate to-day, I reject such associations ; I repudiate and resent such injurious imputations. The courage, devotion and generosity which our soldiers displayed in camp and on the march, in hospital, in battle and in prison pens, were as much higher and holier than the mean virtues which make a man merely respectable in common life, as the heavens are higher than the earth. Some of these men did deeds that would shame the heroes of the revolution. They suffered and bravely endured pains and trials that put them on a level with the martyrs of the Christian faith. They had cut no great figure, some of them, at home ; but they looked well enough, standing there on the perilous edge of fight. Society, with its petty cares and selfish interests, had found no place for them, but they found their own place in the deadly danger of the nation. They had never done very well for themselves, but they knew how to do and dare and die for country.

War affords the surest and most searching test of character. I have said that two men may live near neighbors at home for years, yet neither have occasion to ask what it is a pain to the other to give. But two men never made a march in file, or went through a tour of picket duty together, or moved into action shoulder to shoulder, but if one was a pig the other knew it. No well trained hypocrisy can stand against the revelations of a campaign. No superficial polish of manner can hide selfishness, coldness or cowardice here. No mere habit of politeness will conceal the real disposition of the heart.

You know how thousands of our soldiers met this test; how cheerful in hardships, how faithful to duty, how kind and true to comrades, how patient and uncomplaining in sickness and wounds, how peaceful and brave in death. Men little known before, and that perhaps not very favorably, exhibited such valor, fortitude and faith as made all beholders wonder. Deeds of sacrifice and devotion were performed by rough and untaught men, which shame all history and romance. The beautiful act of that star of chivalry upon the field of Zutphen was repeated a thousand times during our war by men who never heard the name of Sidney. Men uncouth in manner and not particularly correct in life, preferred the claims of others, even at the very table where mangled limbs were to be cut away by the knife of the surgeon; they shared with strangers the scanty crust which was thrown to them to prolong the agonies of starvation; and around many an unplaned board in a rebel prison was exhibited a courtesy such as never graced the dinner of an emperor.

Perhaps I cannot give a better idea of the kind of man I have in mind, than by mentioning a gallant fellow who lay next, or next but one, to me in the hospital of Libby prison, an officer of the 1st Michigan sharpshooters — a regiment, by the way, commanded by a North Brookfield soldier, Col. Charles Deland. This man was shot through the leg, and through both shoulders,

in one of the September fights, so that on whichever side he lay
he pressed a hot and angry wound. Yet for weeks together I
never heard his voice except in answer to a question. All the
time he was in hospital I never heard him utter a groan. He
never made a complaint. I never even knew him call an
attendant to smooth his pillow or bring a glass of water. One
day, however we left Richmond together. My friend, his
wounds still unhealed, was taken off his bed at six o'clock and
carried out to the ambulance, jolted for a mile over paved
streets, then laid down on the deck of a steamer to lie there until
noon; then taken up again on a stretcher, put ashore, lifted into
an ambulance (a Yankee ambulance this time, thank God!)
driven a mile and a half, stretchered again, and finally, at five or
six o'clock in the evening, put on board the good steamer "City
of New York," his day's work done, a pretty hard day's work
for a well man, let alone one with three bullet holes in him.
Happening soon after to go down on to the lower deck of the
steamer, I was arrested on the stairs by a fearful groaning below,
and, stooping down, could see that it came from my silent,
patient friend of the hospital. You may imagine that I stopped
short in something like horror, for when such a man took to
groaning, be sure it meant intolerable agony. In a moment
more the groaning ceased, and I went to his side. To an inquiry
how he felt, he replied very cheerfully. He had got very tired,
he said, lying all day on the side on which he had only one
wound, so he had tried for a few minutes to lie upon the other
in order to rest himself; but had been obliged to give it up, it
had hurt him so. Now, my friends, that kind of spirit was not
rare in the patriot army, and you must not wonder that those
who saw it exhibited are inclined to set it higher than the
"rascally virtues" of peace, and the prim respectabilities of New
England life: that we can forgive a great deal of youthful wild-
ness and folly, provided that when such tests of manhood came,
they were met with fortitude and self-forgetfulness like that of
the Michigan sharp-shooter.

Nor shall we justly remember these men if we call them to mind simply as they were when they went out from among us. There was not one of them that faithfully served his country and courageously followed the flag, upon whom a change did not pass, greater than that which is usually wrought by the experiences of a score of years. Many of them boys, they passed at once from the gristle to the solid bone of manhood. Thoughtless and even idle, as some of them had been, they were brought face to face with trials from which mature men might shrink, yet acquitted themselves in all respects nobly. The change of character which followed upon these experiences we shall do wrong to overlook. A year, a month, a week is sometimes a very short time; sometimes again it embraces half the facts of a long life. Boys over night rise up men. Vacillation gives way, once for all, to steady purpose, frivolity to earnestness, the spirit of self-indulgence to a capability of endurance and of effort almost passing belief. A single battle has done this for many a soldier; changed the whole tone of his being, and made him in every respect a different man. No one who has ever served with troops will deem this fantastical, or merely possible. I do not mean to assert that such a change passed upon all our soldiers, or that the change was never for the worse; but no man ever commanded a company who has not seen more than one thoughtless, idle boy rise to a splendid and resolute manhood under the first touch of war's trials and responsibilities.

So would I believe of every soldier here represented. I would assume that, as others surely did, he found all the noble possibilities of his nature forming into character under the heroic excitements and the magnificent opportunities of a war of patriotism and a war of liberty. Nay, my hope and faith would never leave him, though defeated by melancholy and mortifying evidence, down to the very moment when disease stretched him on the scanty pallet of the hospital, or, struck by the fatal bullet, he fell to gasp away his life on the trampled battle-field. What has not an hour wrought, an hour of such thoughts, such feelings as crowd themselves into the dying moments of a man? Ask your army nurses how many wounded men, how many dying of disease, but conscious and composed, they ever heard repine at their lot or regret their choice. Looking death calmly in the face, leaving all the hopes and joys of life, without even the consolation of bidding adieu to friends, these men then if never before, realized the nobleness of duty and of sacrifice; and when life was sweetest, because just about to depart, they resigned it without a murmur. Nay, though the fatal bullet had passed through heart or brain, I would not give up my faith and hope. Do you remember what some one says in Mrs. Stowe's Minister's Wooing of the sudden death of a sailor, that from mast-head to deck was time enough for divine grace to operate in? Then let us not believe (why should we? what right have we?) that one of these men fell in his place without a thought worthy of his immortal spirit, without an impulse of devoted patriotism, without, once for all, consenting to his own death for country and for liberty.

My friends, of the thirty-one soldiers whose names are written on this shaft, but seven lie buried with our village dead. Of the rest, some were accorded the burial, hurried and rude, yet not without honor, which comrades give to comrades between two days of desperate battle. Others were thrown unregarded into the sorrowful wide trenches which are dug upon every field for the dead of the vanquished army. Others, alas! lie in unmarked graves, just outside the fearful stockades in which their lives wasted away through sufferings of body and of mind to which the annals of human cruelty hardly furnish a parallel.

But wherever our brave boys lie, whether beneath a turf daily strewn with flowers and watered with tears, or in undistinguished graves on southern soil; whether beneath the monumental marble, or in the ghastly pits of the battle field, like Shaw, "buried with his niggers"— we know that they are marked and guarded by Him who is the resurrection and the life, and who, out of the mingled dust of friend and foe, of young and old, of white and black, shall build up again the perfect frame of each, to be no more subject to decay, disease and death.

Peaceful be their repose! Joyful their awakening! Perfect and unalloyed the fruition of their renewed and immortal life! Though we cannot watch over their long sleep, we know they are not unattended.

> " By fairy hands their knell is rung;
> By forms unseen their dirge is sung;
> There Honor comes, a pilgrim grey,
> To bless the turf that wraps their clay;
> And Freedom shall awhile repair,
> To dwell a weeping hermit there."

GEN. DEVENS' ADDRESS.

FELLOW CITIZENS:

With the sound of the noble oration from my comrade and friend, to which we have just listened, still vibrating on our ears, and its sentiments still holding their first impression on our hearts, I feel that I can add little that would interest you, yet I will not disguise my gratification that by a contingency which I could not have anticipated when I received your invitation, which I then felt compelled to decline, I have been enabled to be present on this deeply impressive occasion, and with you to bring my tribute to, and lay my wreath upon, the memorial you have this day consecrated to the brave departed.

It has given me, also, sincere pleasure to feel again, to-day, the cordial grasp of the hand of so many who were my own comrades in the conflict through which we have passed, to meet again the patriotic citizens of this prosperous town, which has given so lavishly of its blood and its treasure, and especially to greet those of them, survivors of the war of 1812,* who so fitly grace your front seats at this gathering. Soldiers of an earlier generation, they have come to bear their testimony to the valor and worth of the generation which has succeeded them, and on my own behalf, and on that of all my comrades, I pay them the homage of our most affectionate respect and regard. " Better and braver men " said the late Lieut. Gen. Scott, in my

---

* *Veterans of the War of* 1812.—Dea. Joseph A. Moore, Daniel Tucker, Parker Johnson, Cheney Dewing, Anson Gitlin, Thomas A. Harwood, Perley Ayres.

presence, "than Massachusetts sent to the war of 1812, no general ever led on the field of battle."

The military history of Massachusetts is a long and honorable one, and they that were her soldiers of 1861, may boast of a brave and true lineage, for they have a right to claim their descent through the soldiers of 1812, through the soldiers of the Revolution, through the soldiers who, twenty years before the Revolution, carried the old Provincial flag of Massachusetts, side by side with the great British ensign, up the heights on the day when Wolfe stormed Quebec; back to the stern Puritan soldiers who, in those days when Brookfield was a frontier post, with the ploughshare in one hand and the musket in the other, maintained their conflict with the inhospitable climate, the rugged soil, the murderous savage, and laid broad and deep the foundation of a truly free commonwealth. It is enough for the soldiers of the war of the rebellion, if it be admitted that in their hands the white standard of Massachusetts has suffered no spot or stain of dishonor, and if they are acknowledged as the legitimate descendants of such a race of men, and are recognized as the "bronze recast of the old heroic ages."

We have met to-day, by consecrating this monument to the brave dead who have died for their country, to honor the memory of those citizens who, unused to the trade of arms, might have looked forward to contented and happy lives in the busy work-shops or well tilled fields around us, and yet who did not hesitate to lay aside the occupations of peace at the sacred call of patriotism, and to commit themselves to the shock of battle, appealing to the God of Battles for the justice of their cause. We have met, too, in deep and solemn remembrance of the costly sacrifice which has been demanded of them, to consecrate ourselves anew to the great cause for which they have yielded up their lives, the cause of civil and religious liberty.

Grave and solemn as is the structure we rear, it is not funereal only, for it is intended rather to honor than to weep the dead.

True it is, those whose names it bears will never be remembered by us except with a quivering lip and a moistened eye, for to us they stood in all the dearest and tenderest relations of life; they were comrades and friends, they were husbands and lovers, they were brothers and sons, but the day will come when no tears will dim the lustre of their glory. As the dead are always recalled by us as they were when they departed, as over them time seems to have lost its power, as Warren is to us the same youthful hero that he was as he rushed into the thickest of the fight at Bunker Hill, although nearly an hundred years have passed away since that eventful day, so these will live in their immortal youth long after the clods of the valley shall have pressed us down to our eternal rest.

In that portion of the Roman annals which tells the story of Hannibal, the most formidable opponent Rome ever knew, whose victories, sweeping over the Alps in anticipation of the great achievement of the first Napoleon, carried fire and sword up to the very gates of the mistress of the ancient world, it is related that when a child of nine years old his father Hamilcar, himself a chieftain and a warrior, whose renown has been eclipsed by his greater son, brought him into the temple of the gods, and causing him to hold up his little hands, made him swear eternal hostility to the tyranny of Rome. Let this monument be an altar also, where your sons shall come to swear eternal hostility, not to one grasping power only, but to tyranny in its every shape and form, and eternal devotion to country and God.

Justice and gratitude alike demand that every wise people should neglect no means of impressing strongly on those who were to come after them the deeds of these and such as these whom this monumental stone commemorates. And this not alone that the dead may be honored, but that the living may be animated by their example, and in their own hour of trial may draw inspiration and courage from the noble self-sacrifice of those who have preceded them. How strong and potent in every stage of our great conflict was the influence of our revolutionary history, how much nearer we ourselves seemed to be drawn to the men of that elder day, how inspiring was the feeling that the liberty they had obtained it was our duty to guard, and that that which had been bought by their blood was to be maintained by ours. Such thoughts as these have sustained the soldier in the wet bivouac, in the weary night march, in the stormy fight, and to the lips of many a brave man, lips that were to know joy and grief no more, there has come a smile as he has remembered that he too had trod, and with no unequal footsteps either, in the paths marked out by our great forefathers.

To us the death of these men, all young or in early middle life, seems premature, yet who does not feel that life to be full and complete which so thoroughly has met life's great ends. Who is there, in those moments of lofty aspiration that come to all of us, if he were permitted to choose where he should meet the inevitable which advances so rapidly, would not wish for himself a fate like theirs.

> " In some good cause, not in mine own,
> To perish; wept for, honored, known,
> And like a warrior overthrown,
>
> Whose eyes are dim with glorious tears,
> When soiled with noble dust he hears
> His country's war song in his ears.
>
> Then dying of a mortal stroke,
> What time the foemen's lines are broke
> And all the war is rolled in smoke."

From the fields where they fought the smoke has long since rolled away, great nature has resumed her wonted reign and covers each mound and bastion with her mantle of verdure, while the wheat waves and dallies with the summer winds on the plains once ploughed by the fierce artillery, but the work they have done will not pass away. Whatever may be the anxieties of the present hour, the soldiers of the Republic have left behind them no task which its statesmen and its people cannot easily complete.

Of those here commemorated I may be pardoned if I recollect

how many were of my own 15th Regiment. I call it my own because I was its first colonel, not because it was not better led afterwards by others. This was peculiarly a Worcester County Regiment, and within its limits, although its military designations were the same with all others, yet the companies were more frequently known by the names of the towns where they were raised and had their headquarters before being consolidated into the regimental organization. I can no doubt repeat them all to-day: thus, Company A was the Leominster Company; B, the Fitchburg; C, the Clinton; D, the Worcester; E, the Oxford; F, from the Brookfields; G, the Grafton; H, the Northbridge; I, the Webster; and K, the Blackstone. It had, it is true, many gallant soldiers who did not come from these towns but from those in their immediate vicinity, but they were all of the County and representative of the whole County, for there was no section which did not furnish some brave men to its ranks. Every soldier believes or ought to believe in his own regiment, and my comrades of other regiments will, I am sure, excuse the affectionate pride I feel in what we used to call "the old 15th." They will agree with me that its name and fame did no dishonor to the heart of the Commonwealth, which sent it forth as an offering upon the altar of our country. When a State has been so nobly represented by all her troops as Massachusetts, it is enough to claim that it holds an equal place with any. Tried too by the most terrible test I may be entitled to remember, of the regiments embraced in the Adjutant-General's Reports of Massachusetts, which have separately returned their lists of killed and wounded so that the loss by battle may be accurately known, the 15th Massachusetts has one of the longest and bloodiest lists.

But, fellow citizens, we rear this monument, not only to these and your other brave townsmen whose names it bears upon its granite sides, nearer and dearer perhaps than any others, we rear it also to all the brave, however widely scattered they lie, who have fallen in the cause of country. Rest then, my comrades, where'er " on fame's eternal camping ground your silent tents are spread ;" rest in peace, your labors have not been in vain, you have not died in vain, the cause for which you yielded up your lives shall live and triumph. Memorials like this shall attest our grateful appreciation of your noble self-sacrifice. They cannot be spread too widely, although they stand in every village which was once your home ; they cannot be reared too loftily, though they " rise to meet the sun in his coming," but a nobler monument than these shall yet be reared to you, when through the wide domain of the eleven mighty States which were the scene of this gigantic rebellion, manhood shall be honored and labor shall be rewarded, whether the laborer bear the swarthy hue of Africa or the lighter tint of our own Saxon race, and when peace and order, liberty and law shall maintain unchallenged their firm and rightful, yet gentle sway.

REPORT

SERVICES OF DEDICATION.

Before giving a report of the services of dedication, a brief account of the monument enterprise may not be uninteresting to the people of North Brookfield and vicinity. Very soon after the close of the war a committee was chosen by the town, of which Dr. J. Porter was chairman, to report upon the feasibility of the project and present plans of a monument, who attended to the matter promptly, and reported favorably upon a design of a plain granite shaft, and asked for an appropriation of $2,500 to carry the same into effect. After considerable debate in town meeting, the burden of which was the great debt of the town, together with the hope expressed by some of the citizens that a Memorial Hall might be erected, the matter was indefinitely postponed.

Nothing more was said of the matter, except among returned soldiers, until the first "decoration day" in the summer of 1868, when new interest seemed to be awakened both among soldiers and citizens, and action was soon after taken to place tablets to the memory of deceased soldiers upon the walls of the town hall. To further this plan a fair was gotten up by returned soldiers, which was so generously patronized by the citizens that $500 was placed at the disposal of the monument committee, after defraying the expense of the tablets. Previous to this time a committee, consisting of Charles Adams, Jr., Ezra Batcheller, Dr. Warren Tyler, Wm. H. Montague, E. J. Russell, T. M. Duncan and John Q. Adams, were chosen to present plans for a monument, who unanimously reported in favor of the statue of a private soldier after a model by Martin Millmore, the well known artist of Boston, but the question of expense seemed almost insurmountable, owing to the heavy debt of the town. Notwithstanding, the report of the committee was accepted and an appropriation of $3,000 was made with remarkable unanimity; the balance of the cost beside the $500 contributed from the soldiers' fair, was made up by private subscriptions, mainly by the firm who have given a name and character for enterprise to the town of North Brookfield. It was the design of the committee to have had the monument completed so as to be dedicated on the 17th of September, the anniversary of the battle of Antietam, the day when three of the men whose names appear upon its base went down under the fire of that terrible day; but delays were occasioned over which the artist had no control, and it was not finally completed until December, 1869. As matters historical and biographical are so perfectly set forth in the oration, the committee cannot better describe the services of dedication than by giving extracts from newspapers published at that time.

[*From the Worcester Daily Spy.*]

According to the announcement made several weeks since, the monument raised to commemorate the honored dead of North Brookfield who fell in the war of the rebellion, was dedicated yesterday by impressive and appropriate ceremonies.

The day was a clear, cold and bright one, pleasant as a winter day could possibly be, with the exception of the rough condition of the ground. The town of North Brookfield was filled at an early hour in the day by dignitaries from abroad, members of the Grand Army from the adjoining towns, and citizens. Many of them arrived Tuesday night, and were present at the concert given by Hall's band, of Boston, which also furnished the music for the dedication exercises. But the express train arriving at West Brookfield at eleven o'clock, brought the most distinguished portion of the number present, Governor Claflin and a part of the council; they were met at the station by carriages and conveyed to the scene of the ceremonies, their arrival in the village being announced by the firing of a salute of fifteen guns, in front of the First Congregational church, in which the address was made. The executive party were made the guests of Hon. Charles Adams, Jr., to whose house they repaired for dinner.

The monument, of which our readers have read accounts from time to time, is of New Hampshire granite, of fine grain, and light grey in color. It is a statue of a private soldier, standing at parade rest, in full uniform, with downcast face, suggestive of the whole mournful story connected with the fall of the brave ones whose names are chiseled on the tablet beneath. The statue is seven feet in height, and stands on a plinth eight feet high, on the north side of which is the following inscription:

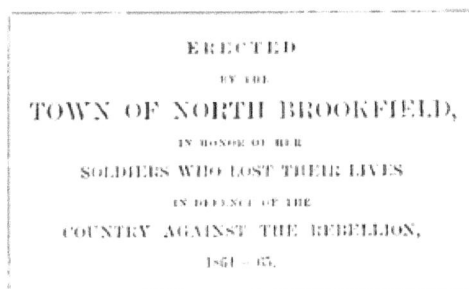

ERECTED
BY THE
TOWN OF NORTH BROOKFIELD,
IN HONOR OF HER
SOLDIERS WHO LOST THEIR LIVES
IN DEFENCE OF THE
COUNTRY AGAINST THE REBELLION,
1861 – 65.

The back of the block presents only a plain surface, while the remaining sides are inscribed with the names of the dead, in the following order:

EAST SIDE.	WEST SIDE.
N. B. Maxwell,	James P. Coolidge,
Peter Devlin,	George S. Prouty,
William Clarke,	Lyman H. Gilbert,
Henry R. Bliss,	Alvin M. Thompson,
Joseph C. Fretts,	Louis D. Winslow,
Charles Perry,	Andrew J. Fisher,
John A. Hughes.	James A. Knight,
Henry H. Moulton,	Lyman Tucker,
Wm. F. Hill,	Albert F. Potter,
Charles H. Ashby,	Wm. Bates.
Albert F. Holman,	David S. Moulton,
Timothy McCarty,	John F. Lamb,
N. S. Dickinson,	Thomas Griffin,
James Henderson,	J. Henry Jenks,
John Gilmore,	Alonzo E. Pellet.
George L. Sherman.	

The monument also bears the name of the sculptor, "Martin Milmore, Boston, 1869."

The monument committee, chosen when the work was first contemplated, were Charles Adams, Jr., Ezra Batcheller, Warren Tyler, Wm. H. Montague, E. J. Russell, T. M. Duncan and J. Q. Adams, and arrangements were effected by them with Martin Milmore of Boston for a monument in granite, like the bronze one designed by him for the city of Roxbury, to be completed by the first of September, though this time was afterwards found to be too short. It was placed in its present position at a total cost of $5,500; $5,000 of that amount was appropriated by the town, $500 was raised by the Grand Army post of the town, and the balance was the generous gift of private citizens.

At one o'clock a battalion formed in front of the town hall, consisting of Grand Army post 51, North Brookfield; post 38, Brookfield; post 36, Spencer; post 82, Warren; post 85, Ware; and a delegation from post 50, Barre, under command of Captain David M. Earle of North Brookfield, and in the order named marched to the residences of Hon. Charles Adams, Jr., and Gen. Francis Walker, headed by Hall's Boston brass band, and escorted the governor and council and the orator of

7

46

the day to the First Congregational church, which was instantly filled on the opening of the doors, hundreds standing outside, unable to get admission.

The monument committee also acted as a committee of arrangements, and superintended the day's exercises most efficiently. On entering the church, the distinguished guests were conducted to seats in front of the pulpit, which was occupied by the orator, Gen. Francis A. Walker, and Rev. Messrs. Dodge and DeBevoise. The band was assigned a place in the center of the front gallery. Hon. Charles Adams, Jr., conducted the ceremonies, and after music by the band and an invocation from Rev. Mr. Dodge, he, on behalf of the committee, consigned the future charge of the monument to the selectmen of the town.

Mr. Adams, spoke as follows :

Fellow Citizens: By virtue of my position on the committee appointed by the town to procure a soldiers' monument, it has been made my duty on this occasion to announce to you the accomplishment, substantially, of the service assigned to the committee — and the announcement is silently, yet more eloquently expressed by the monument itself than it can be by any words of mine — to formally present it to you in behalf of the committee, and to initiate the ceremonies of its inauguration.

Few words are expected from me on this occasion, and I shall endeavor not to disappoint that expectation. Other and distinguished gentlemen are present, I am happy to say, to whom the duty of addressing you has been specially assigned, and to whom I know we shall all listen with great interest.

The town committee of which I have the honor to be a member, was originally appointed to consider the subject of procuring a monument in honor of our deceased soldiers, to present designs and report upon their expense. From a considerable number of monuments, drawings and designs visited and examined by the committee, they unanimously selected the monument designed and executed by Mr. Milmore of Boston, for the citizens of Roxbury; and recommended it to the town, substituting granite instead of bronze as the material for the statue. That recommendation was adopted by the vote of a large majority of the citizens, and the sum of $3,000 voted for the purpose, the committee guaranteeing that no further call should be made upon the town for the necessary balance above that amount. The same committee was instructed to procure its execution and erection. The result of our labors is before you. Now, in behalf of the widows and children, the fathers and mothers, the brothers and sisters of our fallen heroes, who contributed not alone their labors, but their lives, that we, that the nation, might live; in behalf of their surviving comrades; in behalf of a grateful country; in behalf of all posterity, I thank the citizens of North Brookfield by whose patriotic munificence, chiefly, this beautiful and appropriate monument has been erected. To the sculptor whose absence on this occasion I very much regret, whose eye sought out among the ledges of the Granite State the block which contained the statue now before you, whose cunning hand chiseled away the flinty shroud and developed to the light of day the beautifully life-like and historic form, suggestive of the whole story, even without the sorrowful details inscribed upon its base; to him, to Martin Milmore, are our thanks especially due and most sincerely accorded.

It is recorded in the sacred scriptures that the Israelites were directed, when their children in time to come should inquire in relation to the monument erected at Gilgal, from the stones taken from the bed of the river Jordan, "what mean these stones?" to answer, saying, "Israel came over this Jordan on dry land, for the Lord your God dried up the waters of Jordan from before you until ye were passed over, as the Lord your God did to the Red Sea, which he dried up before us until we were gone over." So, fellow citizens, when in time to come you shall lead your children to this sacred memorial, and they shall ask "what mean these stones?" you can answer them, saying, "through a wilderness of two hundred years of slavery more than Egyptian; through the Jordan of a most wicked rebellion, with its red sea of blood, whose waves were crimsoned from the veins of the soldiers here commemorated, did the Lord your God lead your fathers, drying it up before them until they were gone over, and their feet firmly planted on the shores of the promised land of liberty and peace." And I know of no more fitting corollary than that pronounced by Joshua on the occasion alluded to above, " That all the people of the earth may know the hand of the Lord, that it is mighty, that ye might fear the Lord your God forever."

And now to the constituted fathers and guardians of the town, the conservators alike of its morals and of its material interests; to you, Mr. Chairman, and to your colleagues, and to your successors in office, is the care and custody of this beautiful and sacred memento intrusted forever. Please accept the trust now relinquished by the Committee.

It was accepted by Dr. Warren Tyler, Chairman of the Board of Selectmen, in the following brief speech:

Mr. Chairman: It is with much pleasure that I, in behalf of the citizens of North Brookfield, accept this token of respect for our fallen soldiers, and gratitude for those who lost their lives in the cause of human liberty and that the republic might live, and trust that the guardians who are to come after us, together with the beautiful expression of sympathy and pity the granite is made to speak, will protect it from all harm; so that it may tell to generations in the far distant future that we loved liberty and honored the true soldier.

Gen. Walker was then introduced, and proceeded in a most eloquent manner to address the large audience, the strict silence showing the eagerness of those assembled to listen to their townsman who had come from Washington to address them on this occasion. The oration was listened to with the profound attention worthy the effort of the orator.

Following the oration, there was music by the band, after which Rev. Mr. DeBevoise made the dedicatory prayer.

His Excellency Gov. Claflin was introduced at this point, and was warmly welcomed by applause as he rose to address the audience.

REMARKS OF HIS EXCELLENCY GOV. CLAFLIN.

Fellow Citizens: I fully concur in the words of the orator, that this is essentially a soldiers' day, and that those who are not military men, or who were not in the war have no business here, except, indeed, it be to testify their deep sympathy with the sufferers, and to show their remembrance of the promises made to the brave men who have passed away. At the commencement of the war these men were promised that they should be remembered while absent, and that, if they fell and it were possible, they should be brought back to their homes, laid by the side of loved ones, and kept in remembrance in all future time. So far as they have been kept in remembrance by assemblages like these, and so far as our gratitude has been shown by the erection of monuments, so far have we done our duty. But how small is any sacrifice made now, compared to the great and glorious sacrifices made by these soldiers. Monuments in other countries have been erected by the people or by the authorities, in commemoration of some great hero or monarch. No monuments to the memory of private soldiers are carved, because the wars which slew them were not for the liberties of the people, but were waged to suppress liberty and enthral the masses. The late war in this country showed the better instincts of the people. It was undertaken by the oligarchy of the South for the preservation of the vilest system of slavery the sun ever shone upon. The oligarchy failed and the slave is now free. In the future, when the widows made by that war shall point their children to the name of their fathers upon this monument, it may be some recompense to them to feel that their parent died not in vain. We know that nothing we can do will compensate

those noble men who went to war, for the sacrifices they made.
The descendants of these fallen heroes may gather about this
monument and feel honored in having them for their ancestors.
In the future men will look with wonderment on the nobleness
of the men of that grand army, who having fought side by side
and accomplished the work given them to do, returned quietly
to their homes, resuming the ordinary avocations of life, and
never asking assistance except in direst need. They fought for
the liberties and safety of the nation, and when the great task
was accomplished they passed to enjoy the fruits of their
victory. Let us ever keep in remembrance the noble men who
died; let us gather as often as may be around their monument,
and lifting up our hearts to God, thank Him for having given
them such a victory.

The governor's speech was followed by a most eloquent one
from Gen. Devens, published elsewhere. A benediction by Rev.
Mr. Bent, and the doxology by the audience accompanied by
the band, closed the afternoon services, and the members of the
Grand Army repaired to Union hall, where a bountiful collation
had been provided by the ladies.

A committee, consisting of Messrs. E. J. Russell, T. M.
Duncan, Wm. H. Montague and Hon. Charles Adams, Jr., were
appointed and authorized to print the oration, together with
such account of the proceedings as they should deem proper.

In the evening the multitude, or such part of it as could gain
entrance, assembled in the town hall, where speeches were made,
music discoursed, and the governor was subjected to nearly an
hour of vigorous hand-shaking, after which, his excellency Gov.
Claflin, accompanied by Judge Devens and those members of
the council who were present, was conveyed to the station at
West Brookfield, and returned to Boston.

The entire arrangements reflect the greatest of credit on the
committee, who failed in no detail to furnish accommodations
for guests, and see well to it that nothing was lacking to render
all present comfortable and well provided for.

www.ingramcontent.com/pod-product-compliance
Lightning Source LLC
Chambersburg PA
CBHW031812090426
42739CB00008B/1250